CGP makes Handwriting skills sparkle!

Learning to write can be a daunting task. It takes lots of practice to get those letter shapes correct, which is where this CGP book comes in!

There are handwriting exercises for every day of the summer term, including helpful guidelines and plenty of examples to help with letter formation.

Every week there are fun activities to practise that all-important pencil control — perfect for getting pupils confident with handwriting!

What CGP is all about

Our sole aim here at CGP is to produce the highest quality books — carefully written, immaculately presented and dangerously close to being funny.

Then we work our socks off to get them out to you — at the cheapest possible prices.

Contents

Use the tick boxes to help keep a record of which pages have been attempted.

Published by CGP

ISBN: 978 1 78908 827 4

Editors: Andy Cashmore, Sarah Pattison and Tamara Sinivassen.
Reviewer: Juliette Green

With thanks to Gareth Mitchell and Glenn Rogers for the proofreading.
With thanks to Emily Smith for the copyright research.

Cover image and graphics used throughout the book © www.edu-clips.com.

Printed by Zenith Print & Packaging Ltd, Pontypridd.
Based on the classic CGP style created by Richard Parsons.

How to Use this Book

- This book contains <u>60 pages of daily handwriting practice</u>.

- It's split into <u>12 sections</u> — that's roughly one section for <u>each week</u> of the Reception <u>Summer term</u>.

- A week is made up of <u>5 pages</u>, so there's one for <u>every school day</u> of the term (Monday – Friday).

- Each page should take about <u>10 minutes</u> to complete.

- The term starts off by <u>recapping</u> the <u>alphabet</u> and <u>numbers</u>. The rest of the term involves <u>tracing whole words</u>.

- <u>Day 5</u> of each week encourages pupils to practise their <u>pencil control</u>. It involves <u>fun activities</u> such as tracing pictures, along with <u>Stripes the tiger</u>. Colouring-in tasks are also spread throughout the book for <u>extra practice</u>.

- A <u>typical page</u> looks like this:

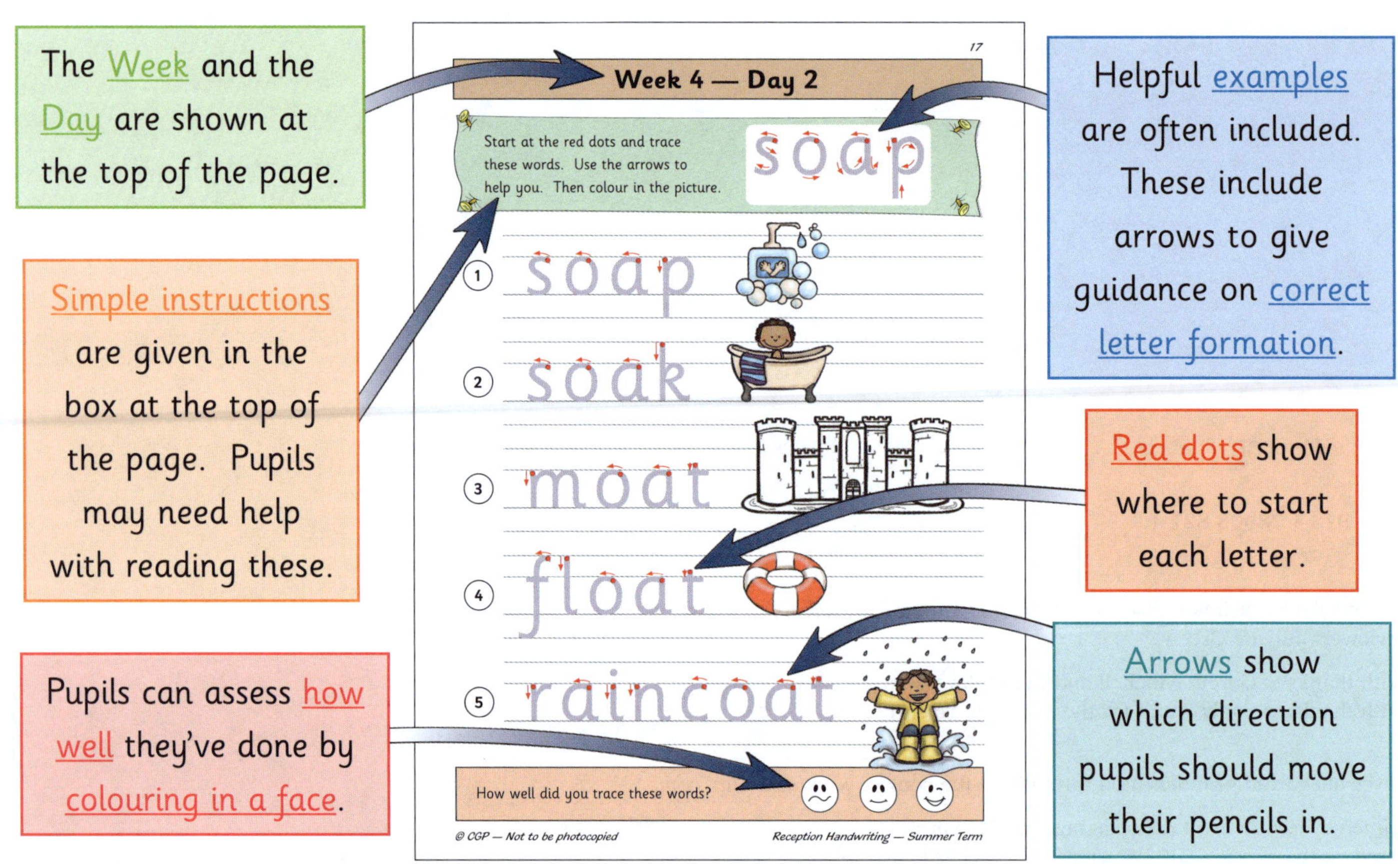

If you are a <u>parent</u> or <u>guardian</u> using this book at home with your child, you should bear in mind that different schools have <u>different handwriting styles</u> (e.g. 'k' instead of 'k'). You should <u>check</u> with the school to see how each letter is written. In this book, some of the letters have <u>flicks</u> at the bottom in <u>preparation</u> for <u>joined-up writing</u>.

Week 1 — Day 1

Start at the red dots and follow the arrows to trace these letters. Keep your pencil on the page for each letter.

1 

2    

3     

4  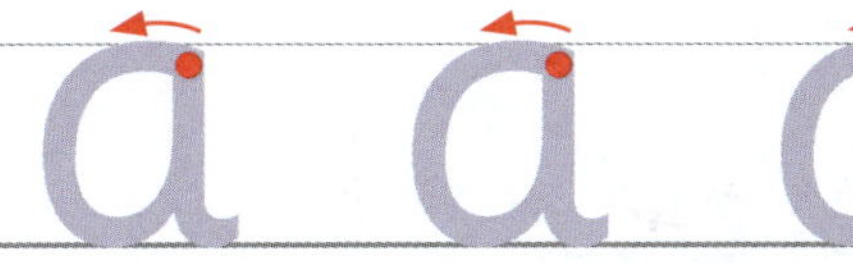  

5     

How well did you trace these letters?   

Reception Handwriting — Summer Term

Week 1 — Day 2

Start with your pencil on the red dots and trace these letters. When you've finished, colour in the picture.

1

2

3

4

5

How did you find these letters?

Week 1 — Day 3

Trace these letters.
Start at the red dots
and follow the arrows.
Then colour in the jet.

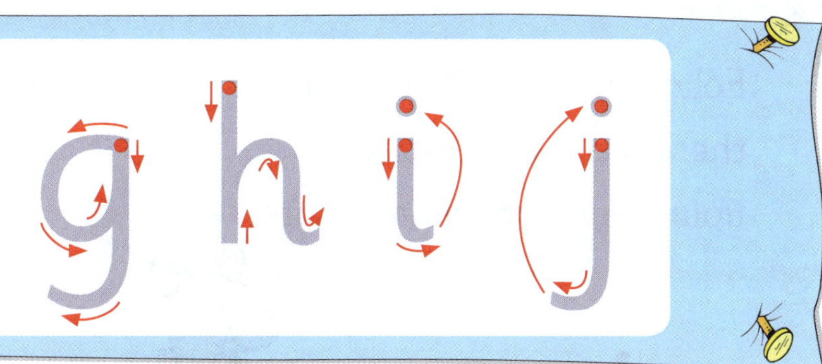

1   g   g   g   g

2   h   h   h

3   i   i   i   i

4   j   j   j

5   g   h   i   j

How did you find tracing these letters?     

Reception Handwriting — Summer Term

Week 1 — Day 4

Follow the arrows to trace these letters. Start with your pencil on the red dots.

k l m

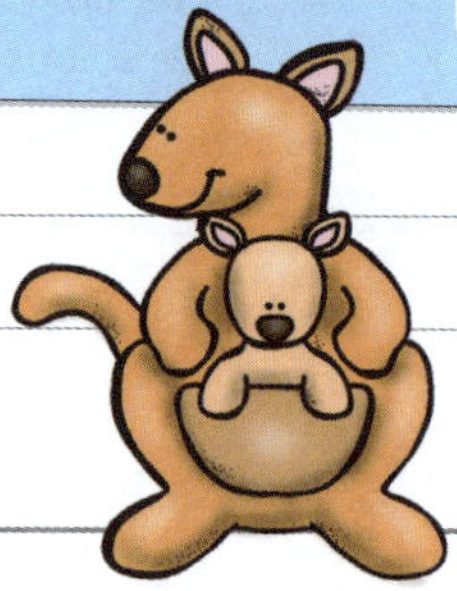

1 k   k   k

2
3 m   m   m   m   m

4 k k k   l l l

5 m   m   m   m

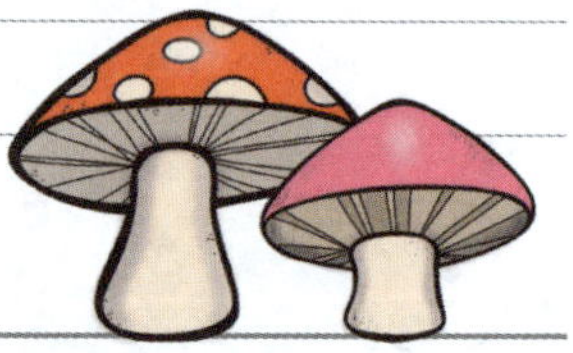

How did you get on with these letters?

Week 1 — Day 5

Stripes has got the letters of the alphabet jumbled up. Draw a line from bubble to bubble to help Stripes put the letters in the right order. The first line has been drawn for you. Then colour in Stripes's friend.

How did you get on with this page?

Reception Handwriting — Summer Term

Week 2 — Day 1

Start with your pencil on the red dots and trace these letters. Then colour in the painter.

1. 

2. 

3. 

4. 

5. 

How did you find these letters?

Week 2 — Day 2

Follow the arrows to trace these letters.
When you've finished, colour in the ship.

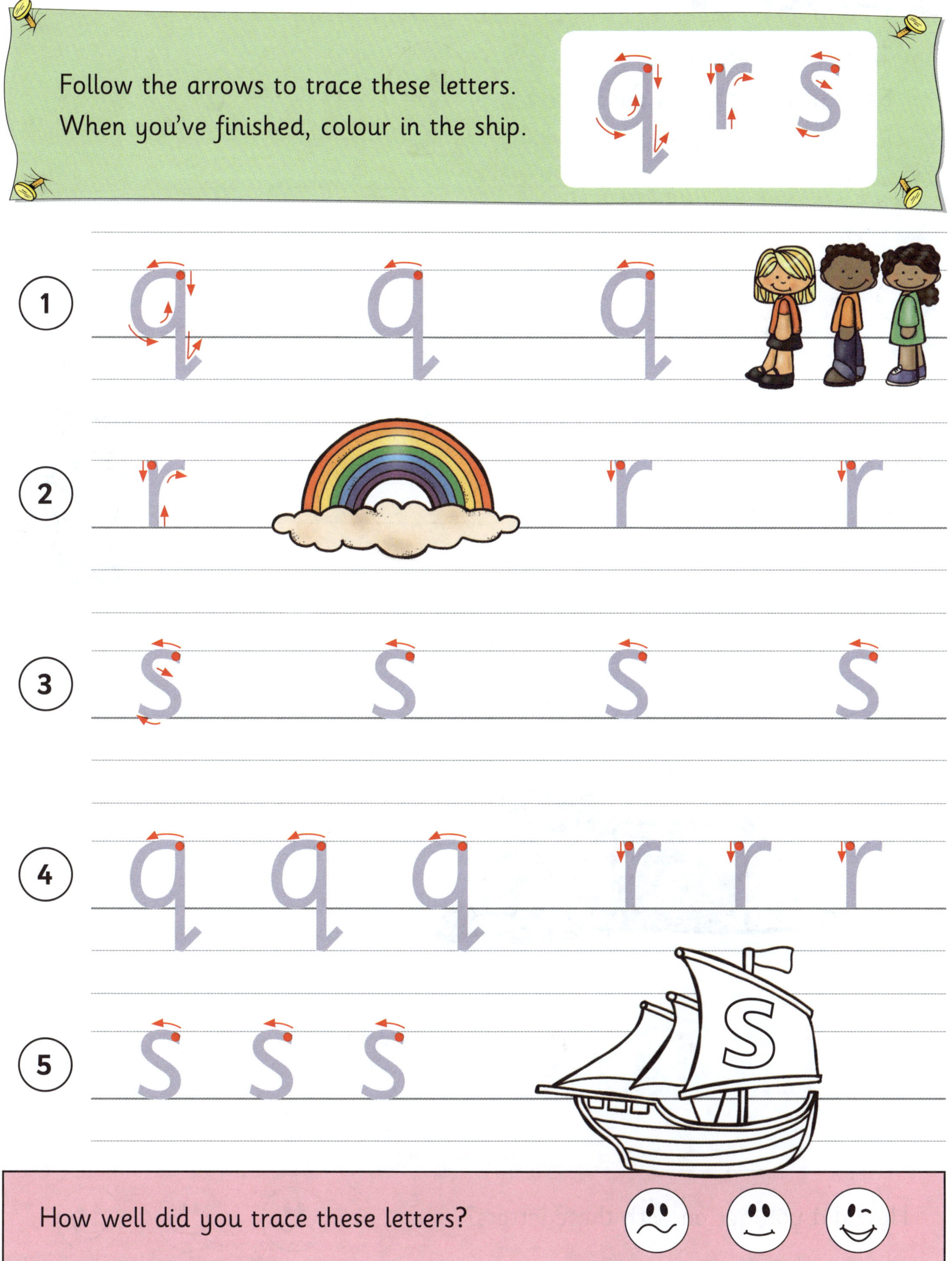

1

2

3

4

5

How well did you trace these letters?

Reception Handwriting — Summer Term

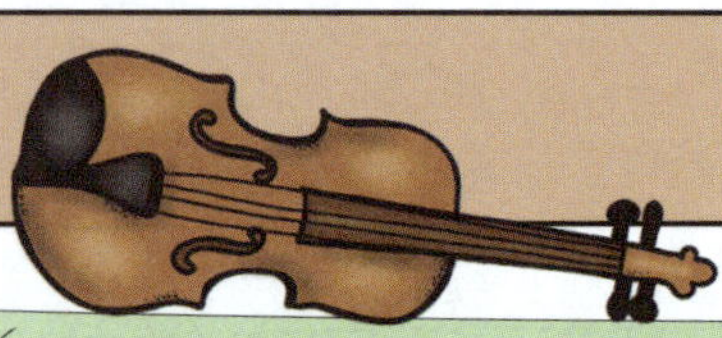

Week 2 — Day 3

Trace these letters.
Start at the red dots and
use the arrows to help you.

t u v

1 t t t t

2 u u u

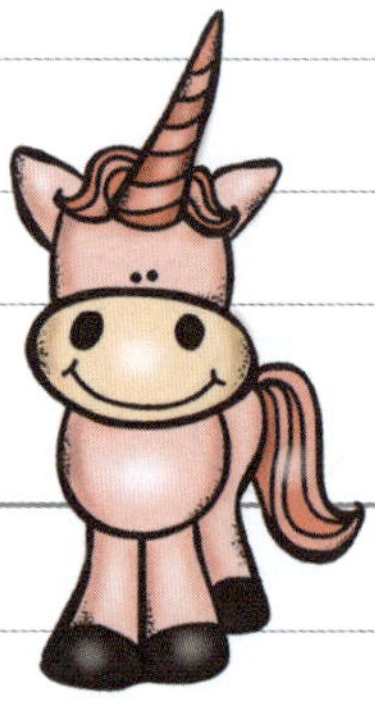

3 v v v v

4

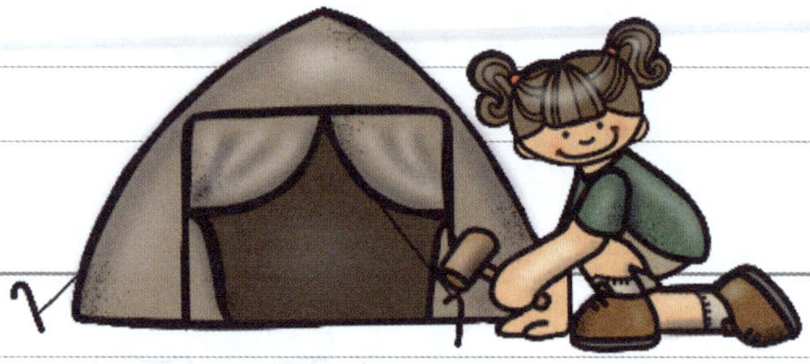

t t t

5 u u u v v v

How did you get on with these letters?

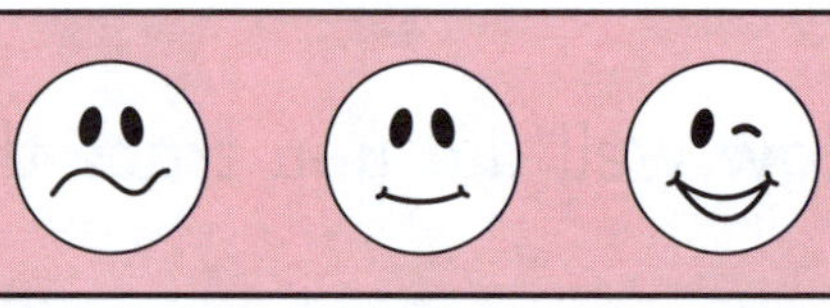

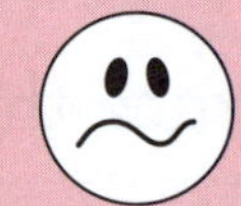

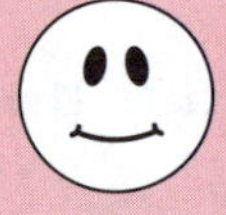

Week 2 — Day 4

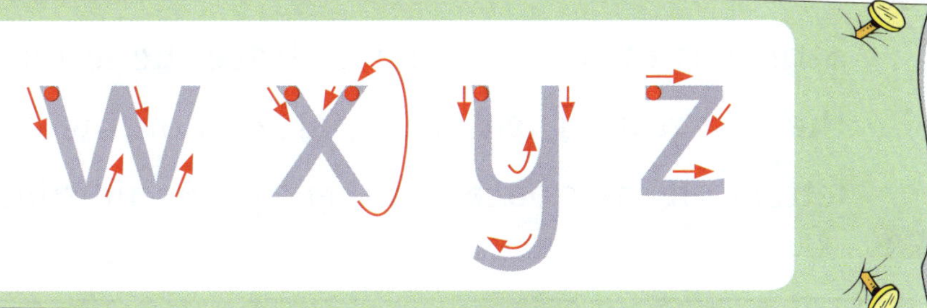

Start at the red dots and follow the arrows to trace these letters.

1 

2 

3 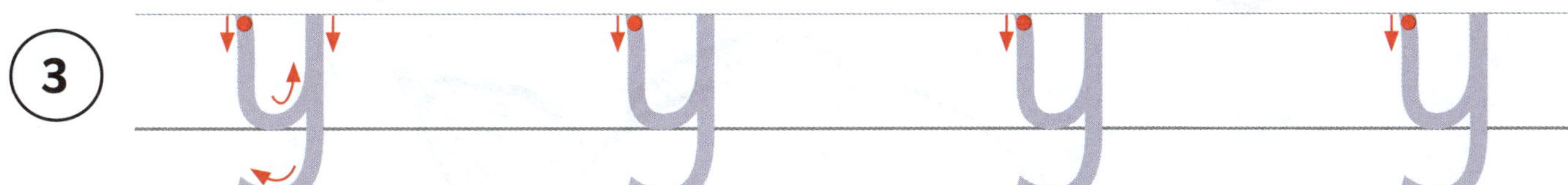

4 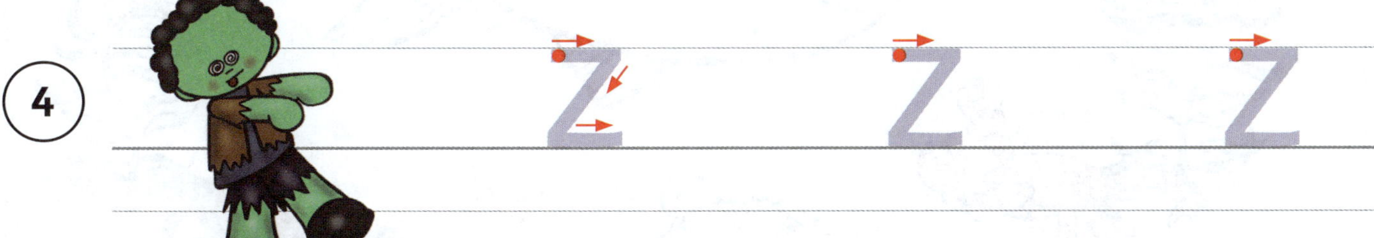

5 

How did you get on with this page?

Reception Handwriting — Summer Term

Week 2 — Day 5

Stripes is at the aquarium. Trace the letters in the pattern on the first fish. Then draw patterns on the other fish using the letters on their backs. When you've finished, colour in the fish.

How did you find this activity?

Week 3 — Day 1

Start at the red dots and follow the arrows to trace these numbers.

0 1 2 3

1

2

3

4

5

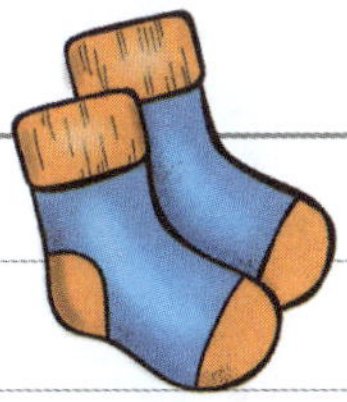

How well did you trace these numbers?

Reception Handwriting — Summer Term

Week 3 — Day 2

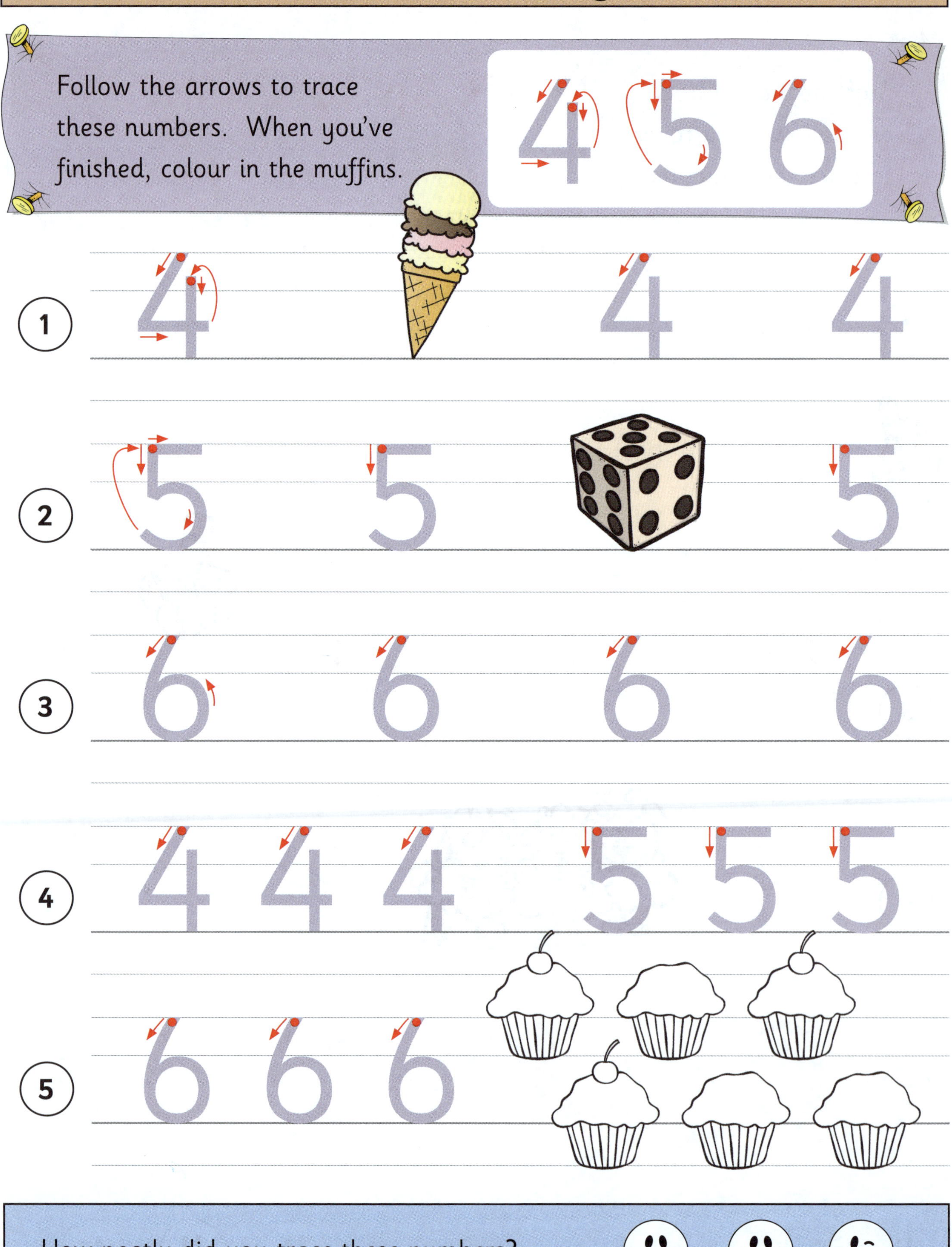

Follow the arrows to trace these numbers. When you've finished, colour in the muffins.
4 5 6
1
2
3
4
5
How neatly did you trace these numbers?

Week 3 — Day 3

Start with your pencil on the red dots and trace these numbers. Use the arrows to help you.

1.

2.

3.

4.

5.

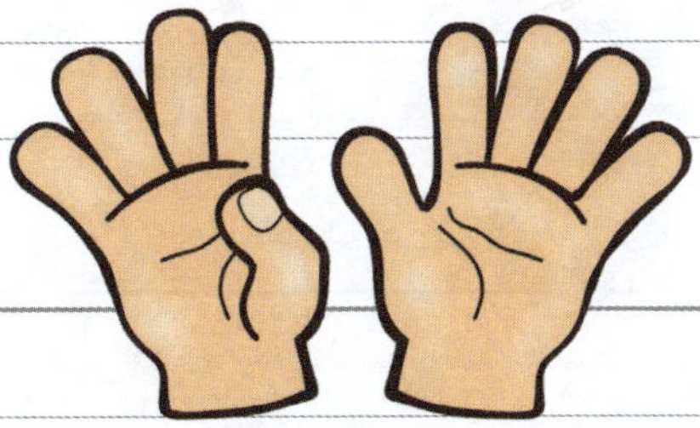

How did you find these numbers?

Reception Handwriting — Summer Term

Week 3 — Day 4

Trace these numbers. Start each number with your pencil on the red dot.
Then circle the number showing the correct amount of each fruit.

1) 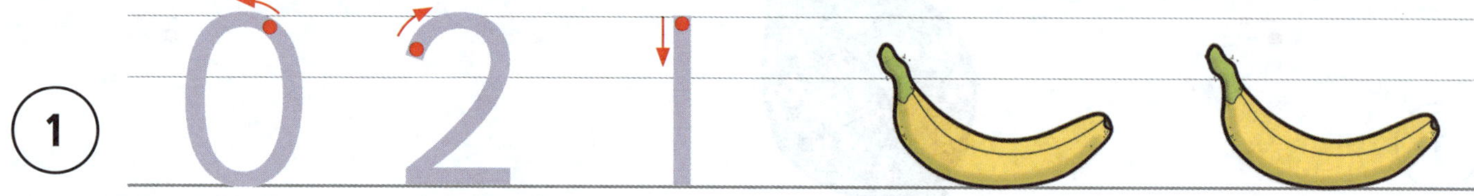
0 2 1

2) 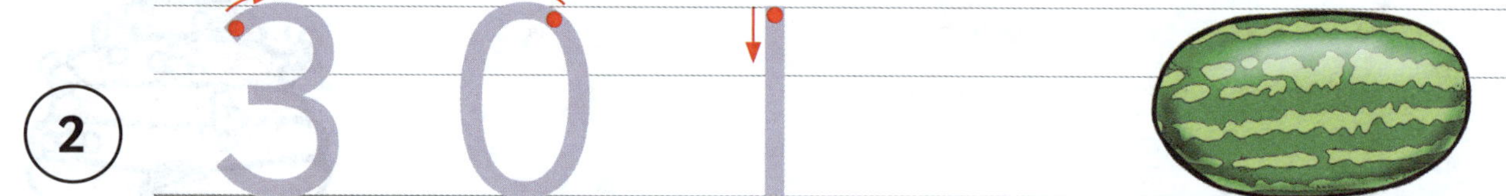
3 0 1

3) 
7 5 4

4) 
4 6 3

5) 
8 9 7

How did you get on with this page? 

Week 3 — Day 5

Stripes is counting animals at the park. Count how many of each animal there are in the park and write the numbers in the boxes. Then colour in the animals at the bottom of the page.

How well do you think you did today?

Reception Handwriting — Summer Term

Week 4 — Day 1

Trace these words.
Remember to start each letter
with your pencil on the red dot.

dear

1. dear

2. tear

3. fear

4. smear

5. beard

How did you find these words?

Week 4 — Day 2

Start at the red dots and trace these words. Use the arrows to help you. Then colour in the picture.

1. soap

2. soak

3. moat

4. float

5. raincoat

How well did you trace these words?

Reception Handwriting — Summer Term

Week 4 — Day 3

Use the arrows to help you trace these words. When you've finished, colour in the bird.

song

1 song

2 fang

3 wing

4 fling

5 strong

How neatly did you trace these words?   

Week 4 — Day 4

①  step 

②  stump 

③  stool

④ 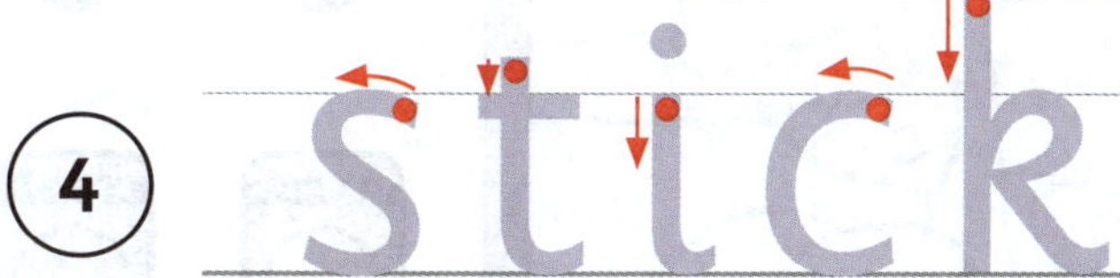 stick 

⑤  stage 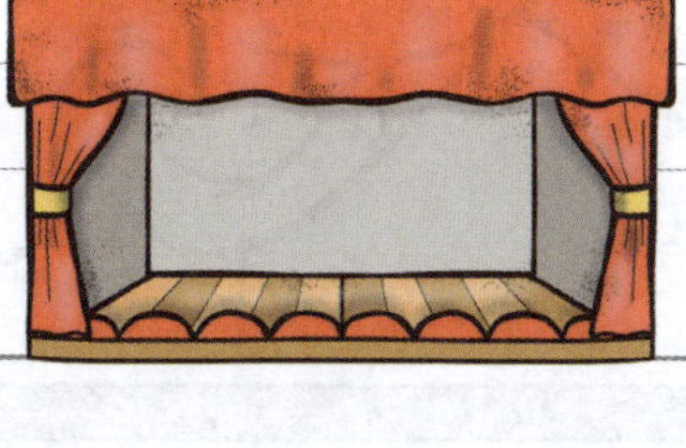 

How did you get on with these words?   

Reception Handwriting — Summer Term

Week 4 — Day 5

Stripes has drawn a picture of a bee.
Use the letters to help Stripes colour in the picture.
The crayons show the colour to use for each letter.

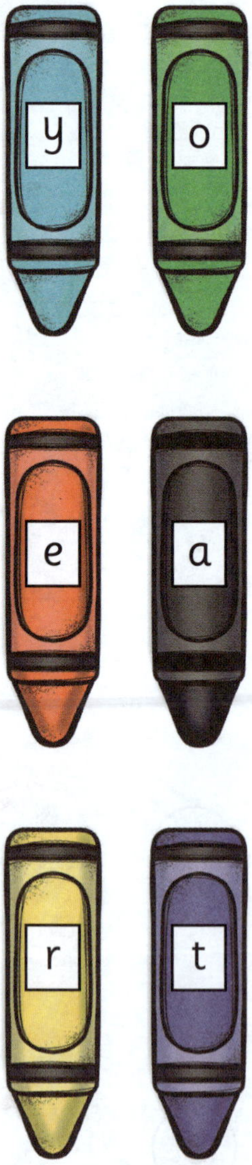

How neatly did you colour in this picture?   

Week 5 — Day 1

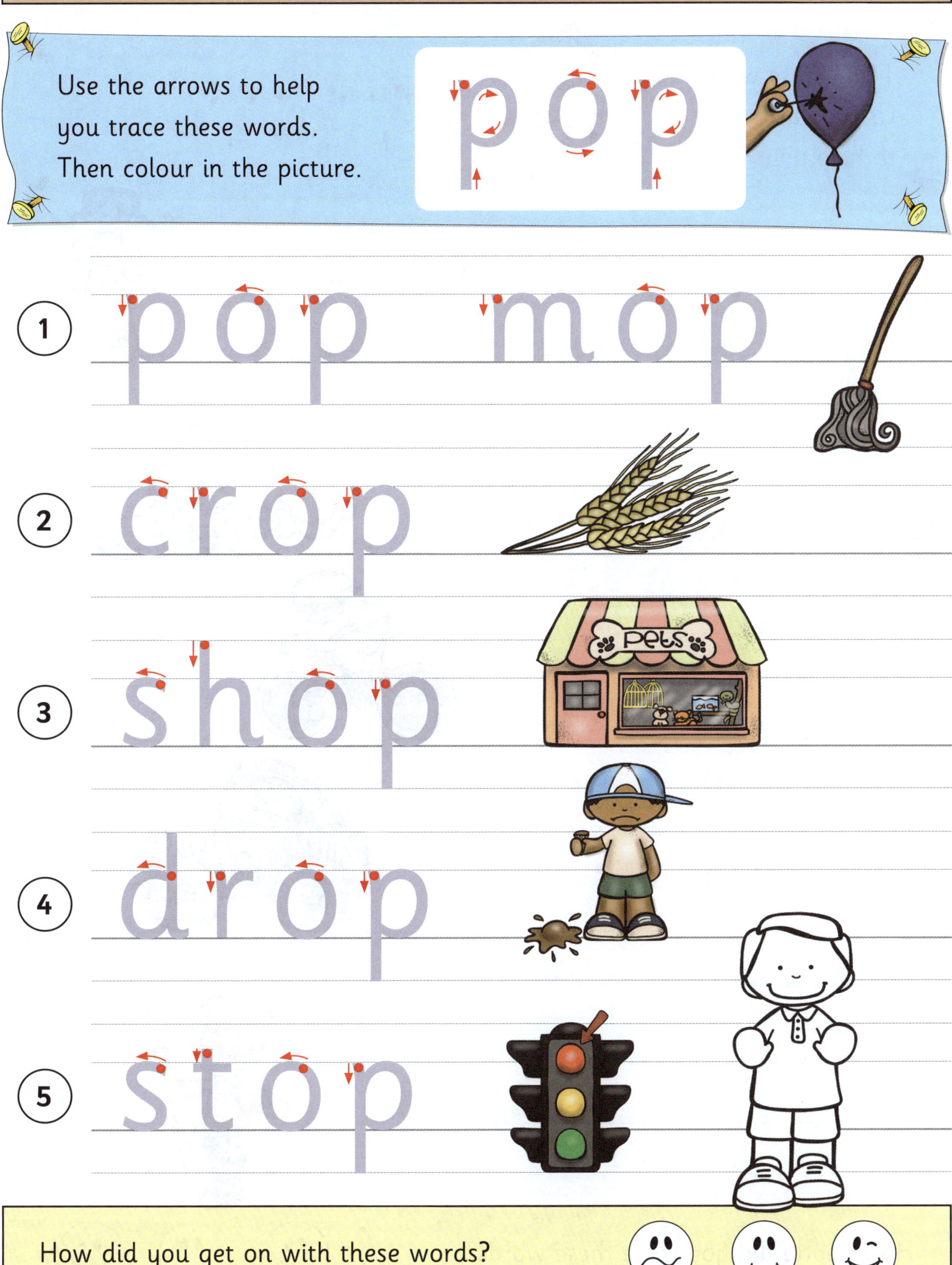

Reception Handwriting — Summer Term

Week 5 — Day 2

How neatly did you trace these words?

Week 5 — Day 3

Start at the red dots
and trace these words.
Then colour in the robin.

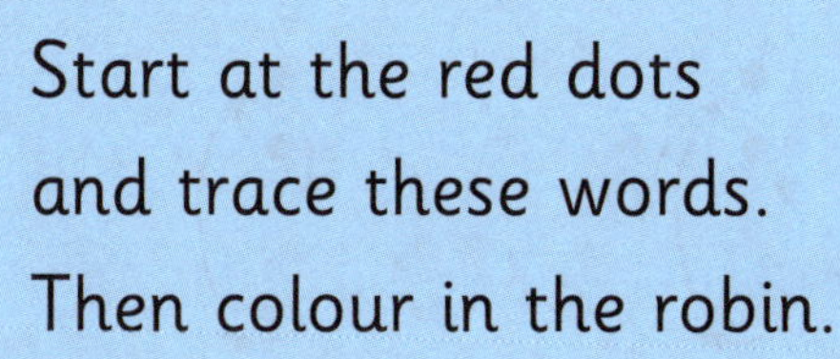

1. bin fin 

2.  chin

3. twin 

4. spin 

5. robin

How did you find this page?

Reception Handwriting — Summer Term

Week 5 — Day 4

Start at the red dots and trace these words. Use the arrows to help you. Then colour in the grapes.

1  kiwi 

2 plum 

3 lime 

4 grape 

5 melon 

How did you find these words?   

Week 5 — Day 5

It's Stripes's birthday. Start at Stripes and draw a line through the maze to the presents hidden in the middle. When you've finished, colour in the pictures.

How did you get on with this activity?

Week 6 — Day 1

Start at the red dots and follow the arrows to trace these words. Then colour in the train.

1 

2 

3 

4 

5 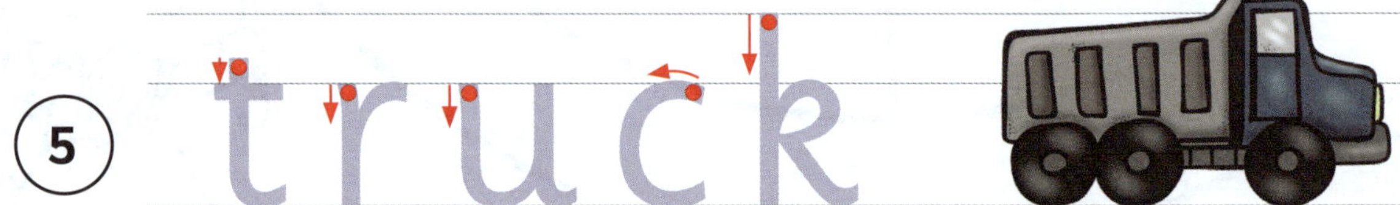

How did you get on with these words?   

Week 6 — Day 2

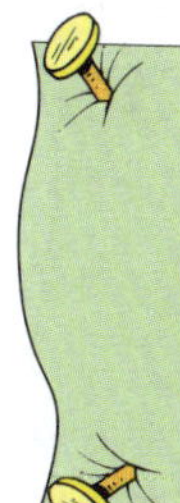

Trace these words.
Use the arrows to help you.
Then colour in the picture.

1.  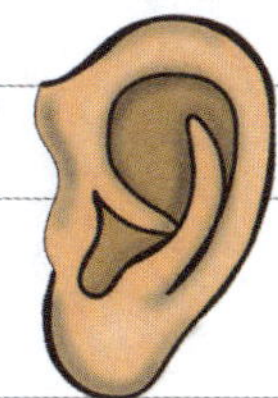

2.  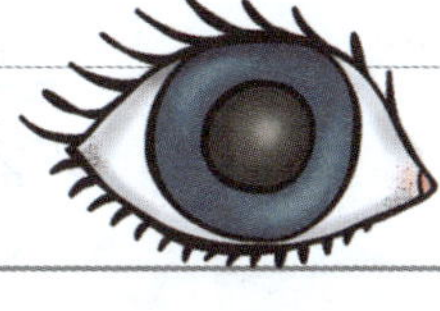

3.  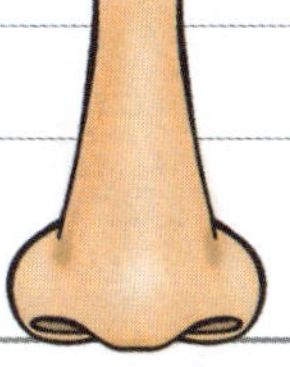

4. 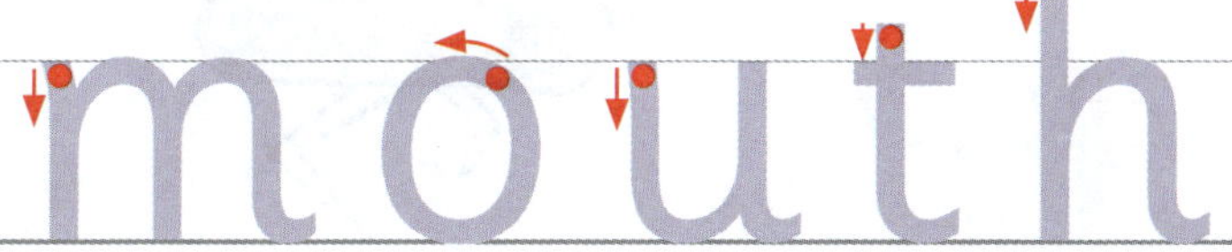 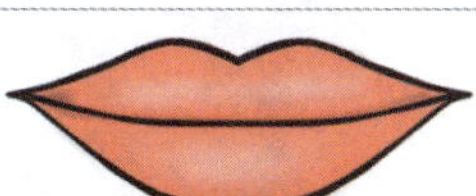

5.  

How neatly did you trace these words?   

Reception Handwriting — Summer Term

Week 6 — Day 3

Follow the arrows to trace these words.
Start with your pencil on the red dots.

1.  ice fog 

2. hot 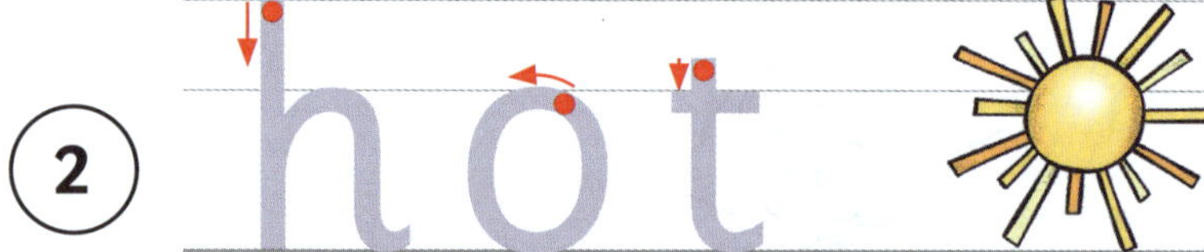

3. wind 

4. storm 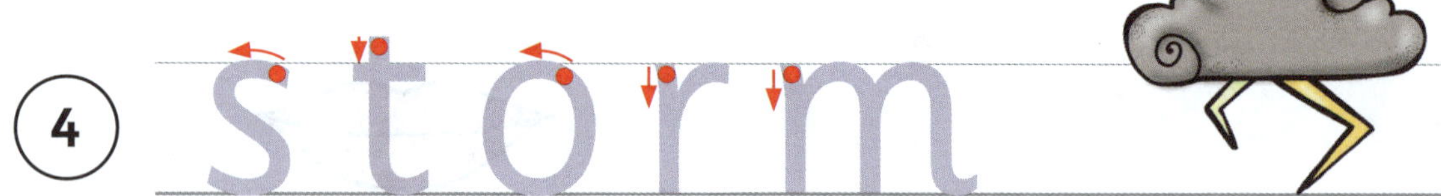

5. clouds 

How did you find these words?   

Week 6 — Day 4

Start with your pencil on the
red dots and trace these words.
Use the arrows to help you.

1  sad 

2 glad

3 cross 

4 shock

5 upset 

How did you get on with this page?

Reception Handwriting — Summer Term

Week 6 — Day 5

Stripes is running in a race with some friends. Trace over the dashed lines to show what place each runner finished in. When you've finished, colour in Stripes's friends.

How did you find this page?

Week 7 — Day 1

Trace these words. Use the arrows to help you.

box

1. box bat

2. bowl

3. skate

4. golf

5. cricket

How did you find these words?   

Reception Handwriting — Summer Term

Week 7 — Day 2

Follow the arrows
to trace these words.
Then colour in the kitten.

key

1. key   kid

2. kind

3. kiss

4. kitten

5. kettle

How well did you trace these words?

Week 7 — Day 3

Use the arrows to help you trace these words.
Start each letter at the red dot.
Then colour in the picture.

1 ant bee 

2 worm 

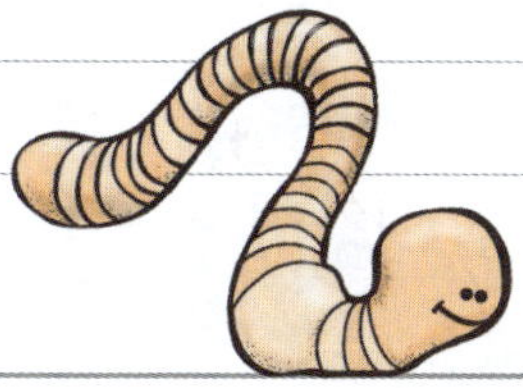

3 slug 

4 spider 

5 beetle  

How neatly did you trace these words?

Reception Handwriting — Summer Term

Week 7 — Day 4

1.  map mud

2. milk

3.  mouse

4. 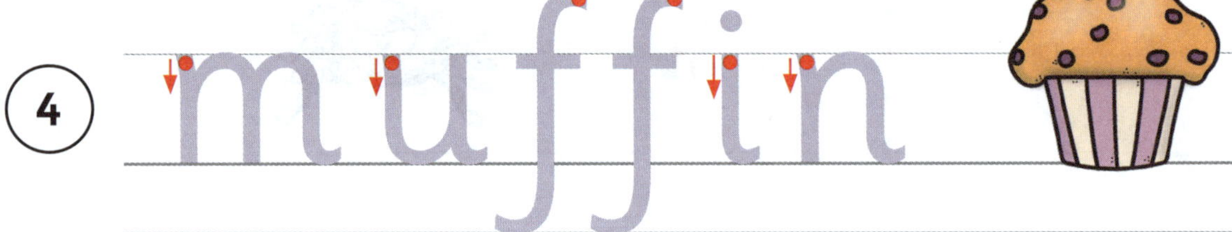 muffin

5.  mermaid

How did you get on with these words?   

Week 7 — Day 5

Stripes has buried some dog treats. The dog digs up all of the bones on its way to the kennel. Draw a path to the kennel that the dog could have taken. Then colour in the dog and the kennel.

How did you find this page?

Reception Handwriting — Summer Term

Week 8 — Day 1

Use the arrows to help you trace these words. When you've finished, colour in the picture.

1.  dip tip

2. skip

3. chip 

4. slip 

5. turnip 

How did you get on with these words?   

Week 8 — Day 2

Start with your pencil on the
red dots and trace these words.
Use the arrows to help you.

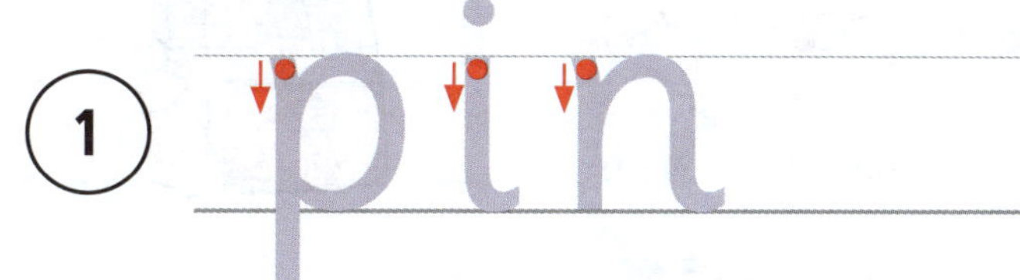

1

2

3

4

5

How did you find these words?

Reception Handwriting — Summer Term

Week 8 — Day 3

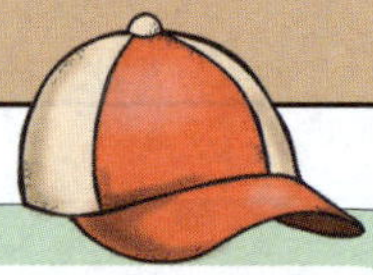

Trace these words. Start each letter with your pencil on the red dot.
When you've finished, colour in the socks.

hat

1. hat bag

2. jeans

3. socks

4. shirt

5. jumper

How neatly did you trace these words?   

Week 8 — Day 4

Follow the arrows
to trace these words.
Start each letter at the red dot.

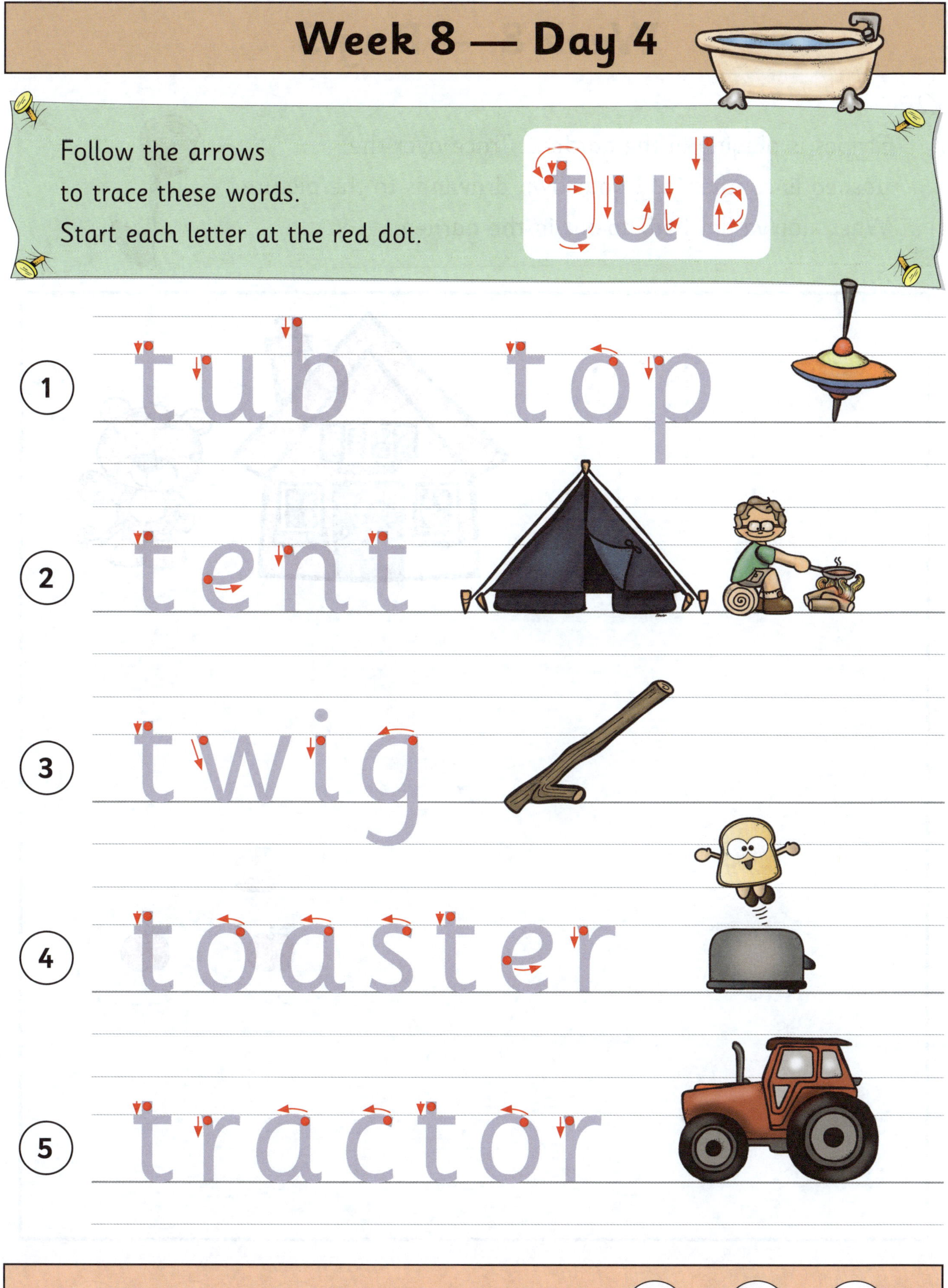

How well did you trace these words?

Reception Handwriting — Summer Term

Week 8 — Day 5

Stripes is playing in the garden. Trace over the dashed lines, then add your own drawings to the picture. When you've finished, colour in the garden.

How did you get on with this picture?

Week 9 — Day 1

Start at the red dots
and trace these words.
Use the arrows to help you.

rich

1. rich

2. munch

3. torch

4. beach

5. church

How did you get on with these words?

Reception Handwriting — Summer Term

Week 9 — Day 2

Follow the arrows to trace these words.
Start each letter at the red dot.
When you've finished, colour in the planet.

1  

2  

3 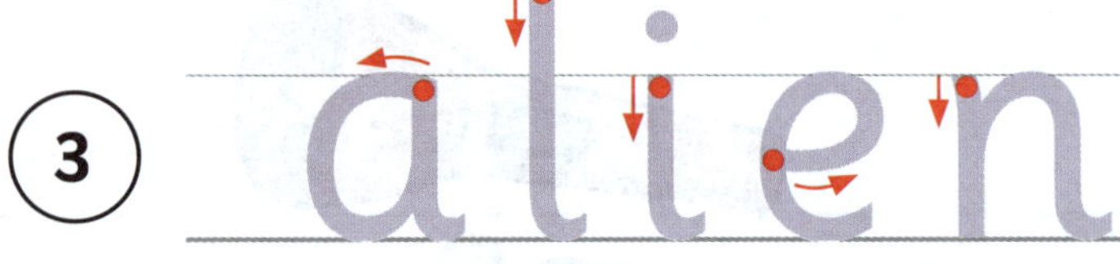 

4 

5  

Were you able to trace all of these words neatly?   

Week 9 — Day 3

Trace these words. Start with your pencil on the red dots and follow the arrows.

1. 

2. 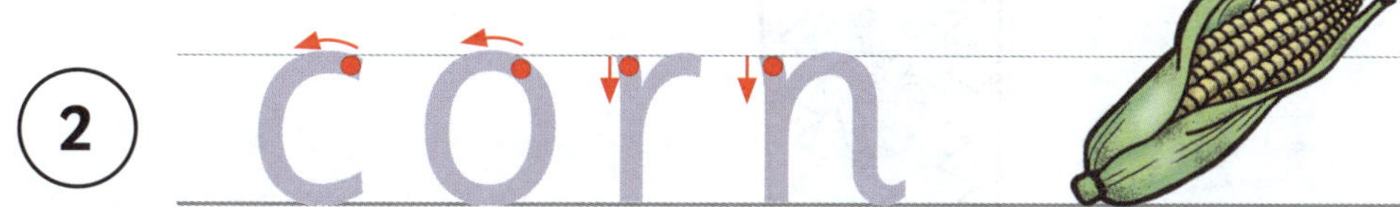

3. 

4. 

5. 

How well did you trace these words?

Reception Handwriting — Summer Term

Week 9 — Day 4

Start at the red dots and follow the arrows to trace these words. Then colour in the cupcake.

1. clap  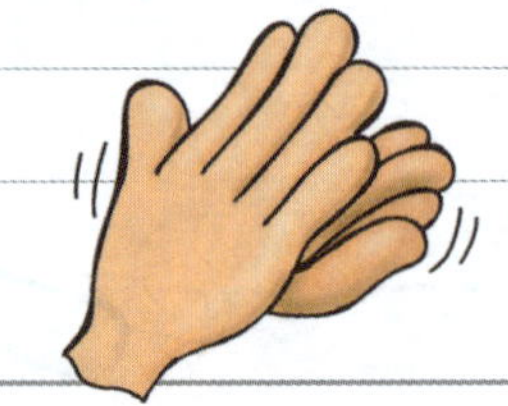

2. card  

3. crown  

4. cactus  

5. cupcake 

How did you find tracing these words?   

Week 9 — Day 5

Stripes is at a restaurant. Trace over the dashed lines to draw the picture below. Then draw some food on Stripes's plate and colour in the picture.

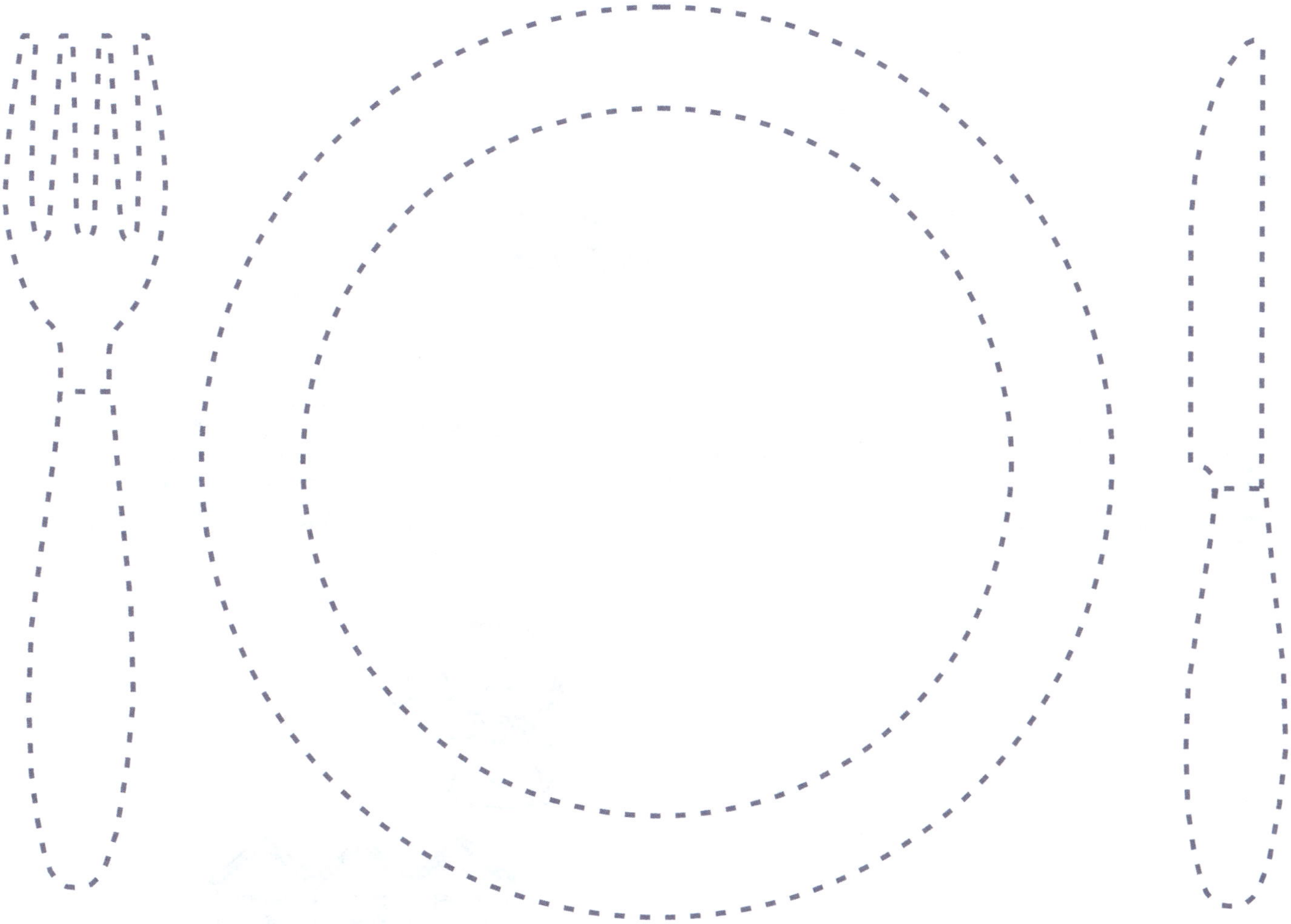

How well do you think you did today?

Reception Handwriting — Summer Term

Week 10 — Day 1

Start at the red dots
and trace these words.
Then colour in the picture.

1. meet 

2. feet 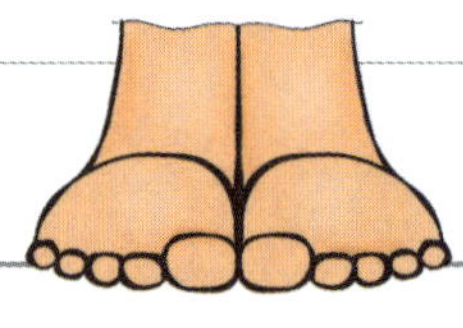

3. sweet 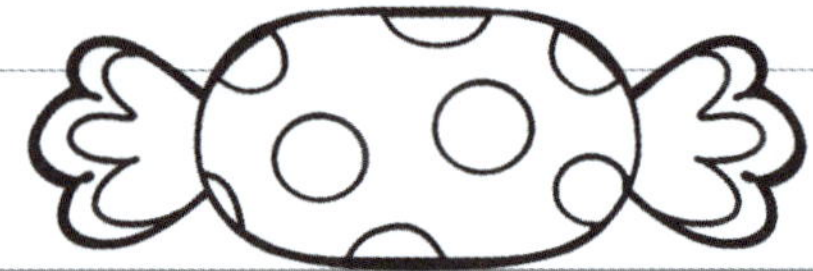

4. greet 

5. street 

How did you get on with these words?

Week 10 — Day 2

Trace these words.
Start with your pencil
on the red dots.

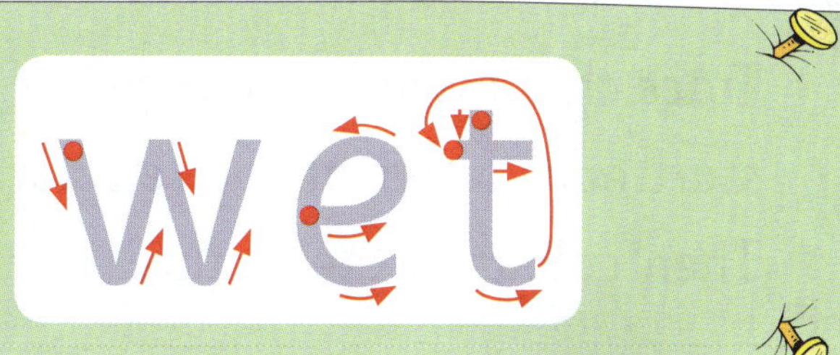

1 wet wig 

2 wink

3 wagon 

4 wizard 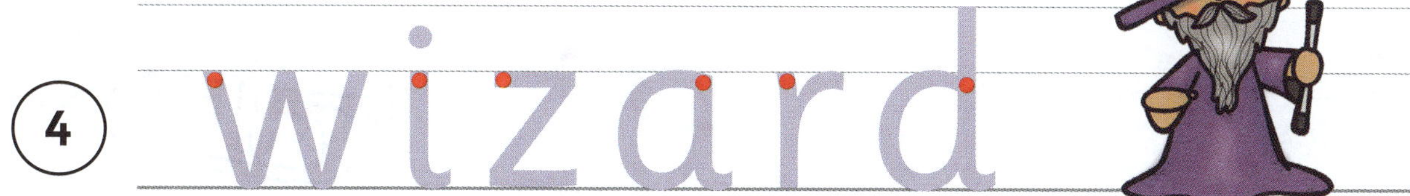

5 wedding 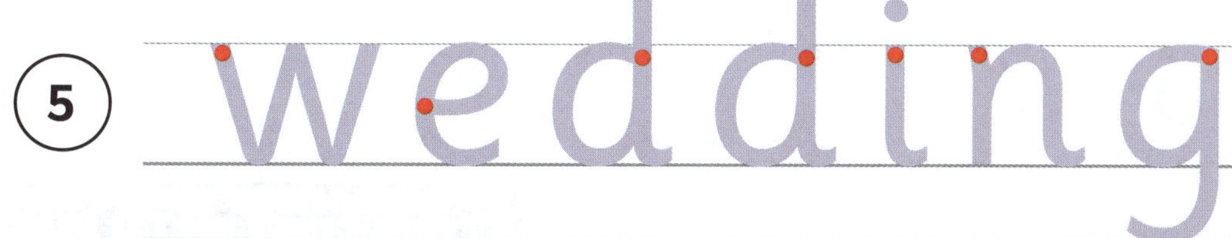

How did you find tracing these words?

Reception Handwriting — Summer Term

Week 10 — Day 3

Trace these words. Remember to start each letter at the red dot. Then colour in the picture.

1 horn

2 banjo

3 singer

4 trumpet

5 keyboard

How well did you trace these words?

Week 10 — Day 4

Start with your pencil on the
red dots and trace these words.

1. nail 

2. drill 

3. ladder 

4. hammer 

5. toolbox 

Did you trace these words neatly?   

Reception Handwriting — Summer Term

Week 10 — Day 5

Draw a line along the path to help Stripes get to school.
Try to stay in the middle of the path and make sure you don't
take Stripes to the wrong place. Then colour in the school.

How did you get on with this page?

Week 11 — Day 1

Trace these words.
Start each letter at the red dot.
Then colour in the picture.

1 hard 

2 soft 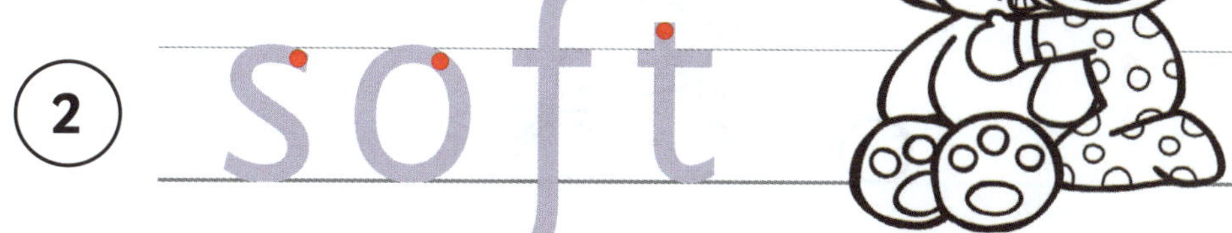

3 flat 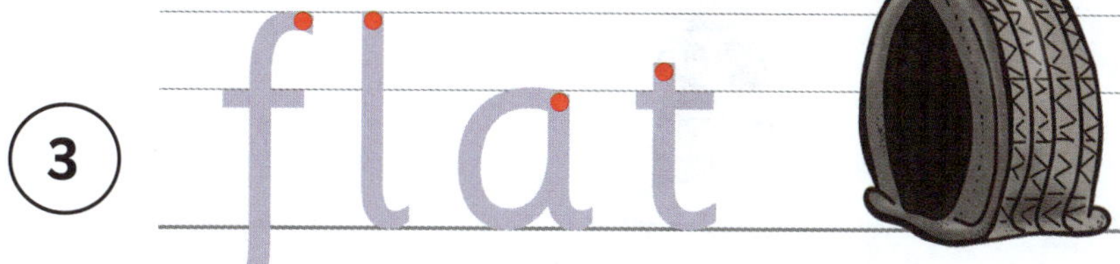

4 steep 

5 sharp 

How did you find tracing these words?   

Reception Handwriting — Summer Term

Week 11 — Day 2

Trace these words.
Then colour in the picture.

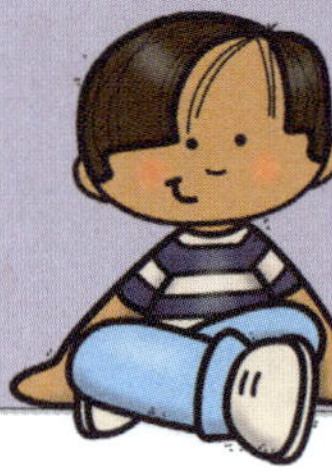

1. sit   eat

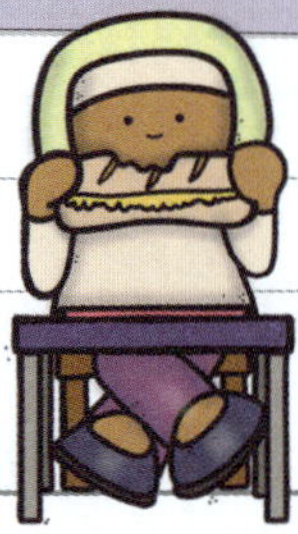

2. play

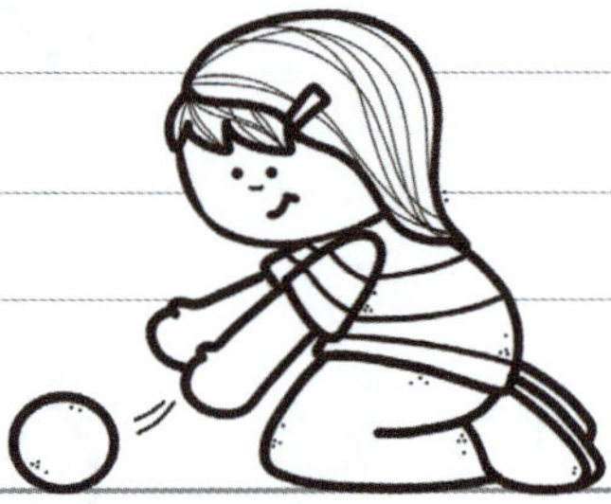

3. drink

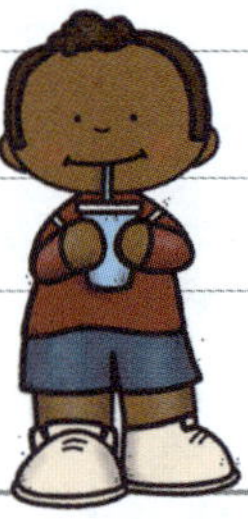

4. brush

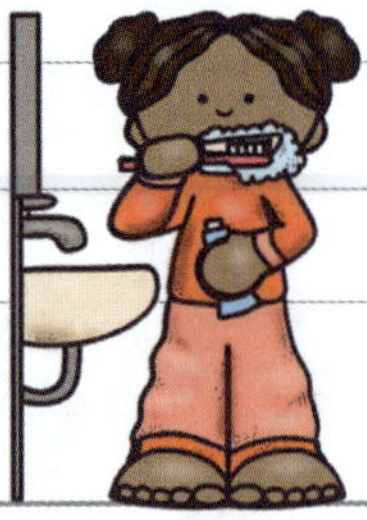

5. sleep

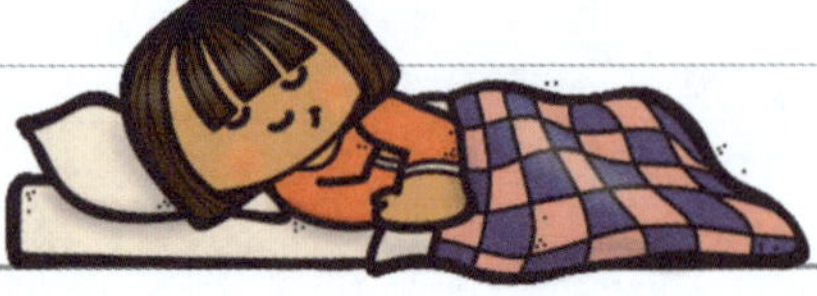

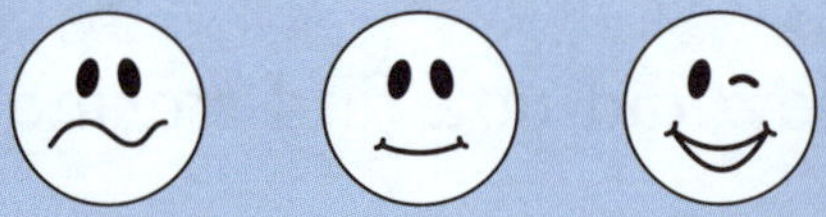

How did you get on with these words?   

Week 11 — Day 3

Start with your pencil on the red dots and trace these words.

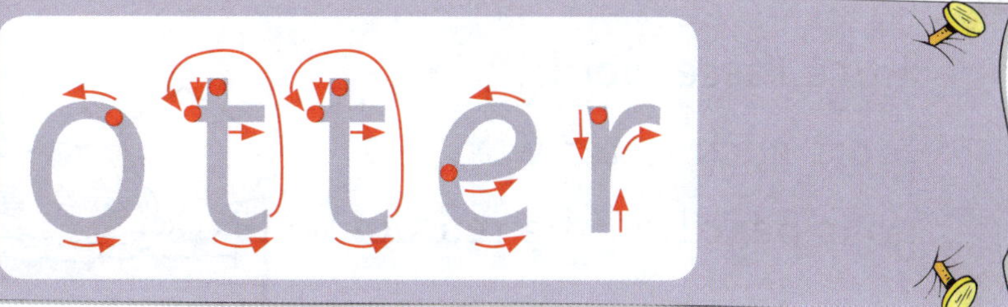

1. otter 

2. panda 

3. skunk 

4. lizard 

5. flamingo 

Could you neatly trace all of these words?   

Week 11 — Day 4

Trace these words.
Start each letter with
your pencil on the red dot.

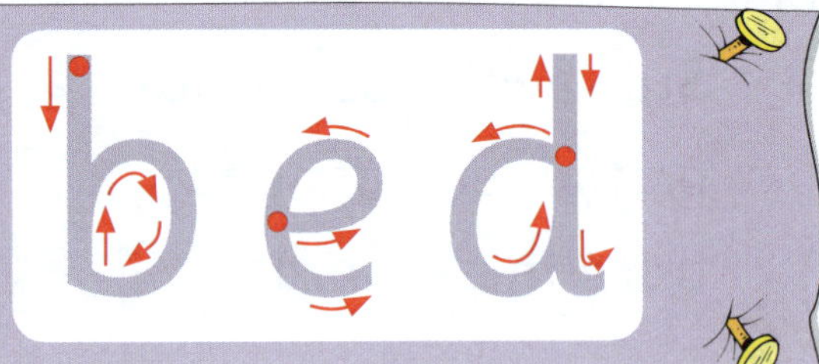

1. bed rug 

2. sofa

3. bunk

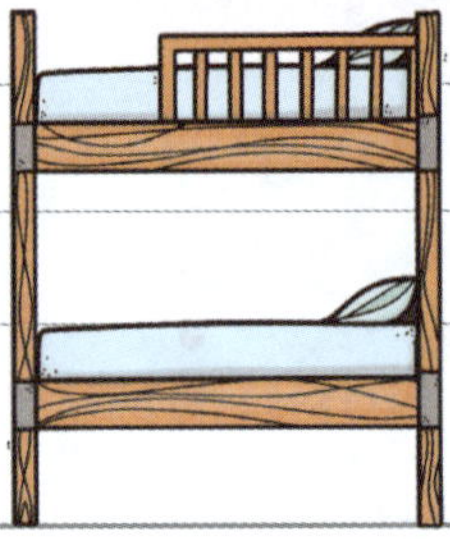

4. bench

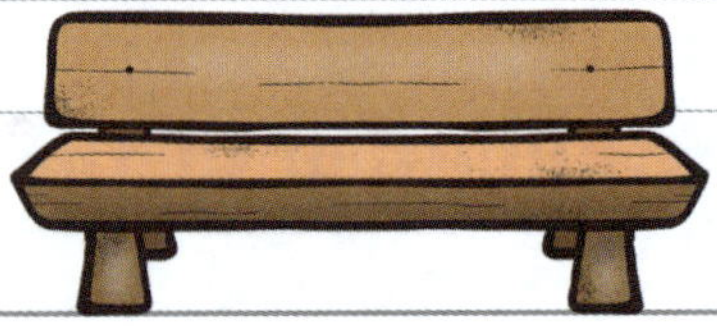

5. bookshelf

How well did you trace these words?

Week 11 — Day 5

Stripes has drawn three shapes on the grids below. Use the grid lines to help you copy the shapes onto the blank grids. Try to keep your pencil on the page for each one. Then colour in the shapes.

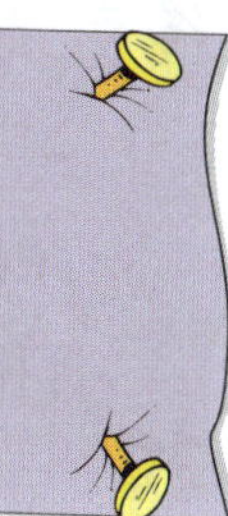

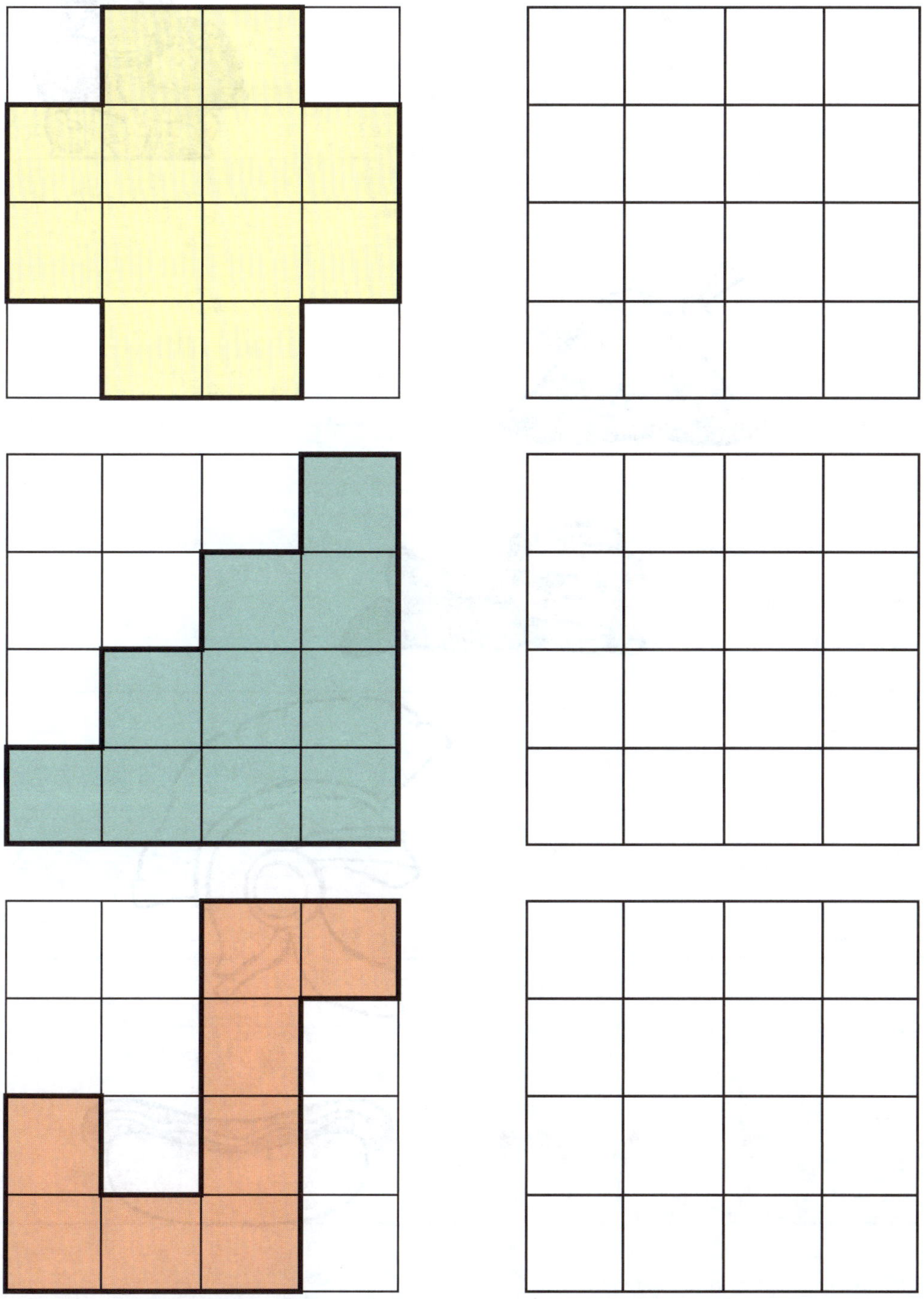

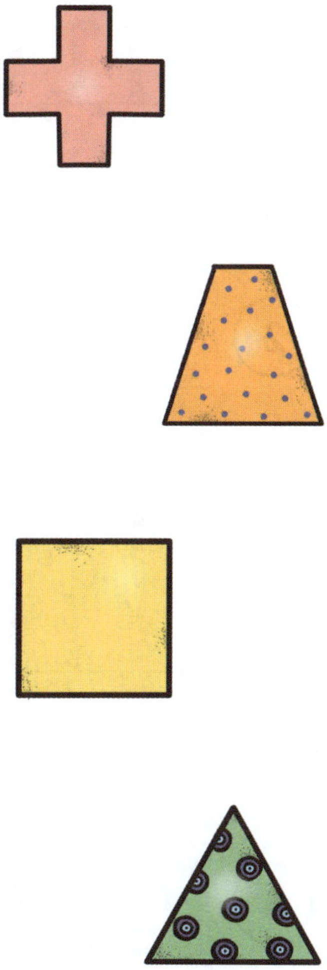

How did you find this task?

Reception Handwriting — Summer Term

Week 12 — Day 1

Start with your pencil on the red dots and trace these words. Then colour in the picture.

1. hen hug

2. hill

3. hero

4. helmet

5. hotdog

How did you find tracing these words?

Week 12 — Day 2

Start at the red dots and trace these words.

jump

1. jump

2. hoop

3. chess

4. scooter

5. frisbee

How well did you trace these words?   

© CGP — Not to be photocopied

Reception Handwriting — Summer Term

Week 12 — Day 3

Trace these words.
Remember to start each letter
with your pencil on the red dot.

1. boot

2. brick

3. butter

4. bucket

5. blanket

How did you get on with these words?

Week 12 — Day 4

Trace these words.
Start each letter at the red dot.

polo

1. polo

2. yoga

3. tennis

4. archery

5. surfing

How neatly did you trace these words?   

Reception Handwriting — Summer Term

Week 12 — Day 5

Stripes is writing a shopping list. Help Stripes by writing the letter that each food starts with in the box.
When you've finished, colour in the food.

How did you find this page?   

ERHWSUR1